inside jogging

for women

wyomia tyus

cbi Contemporary Books, Inc.
Chicago

Library of Congress Cataloging in Publication Data

Tyus, Wyomia.
    Inside jogging for women.

    Includes index.
    1. Jogging—Psychological aspects.   2. Physical
fitness—Psychological aspects.   3. Exercises for
women.   I. Fisher, Barbara, joint author.   II Title.
GV494.T97   1978   796.4'26   77-91181
ISBN 0-8092-7594-5
ISBN 0-8092-7593-7 pbk.

Published by Contemporary Books, Inc.
180 North Michigan Avenue, Chicago, Illinois 60601
Manufactured in the United States of America
Library of Congress Catalog Card Number: 77-91181
International Standard Book Number: 0-8092-7594-5 (cloth)
                                    0-8092-7593-7 (paper)

Published simultaneously in Canada by
Beaverbooks
953 Dillingham Road
Pickering, Ontario L1W 1Z7
Canada

contents

foreword

Many people consider me primarily a competitor. They could be partly right as far as tennis is concerned, but competition is only part of the story. What has really characterized my career is a drive for perfection. No matter what I have undertaken, whether on the tennis court, in tennis administration, or in publishing *womenSports* magazine, my primary drive has been to achieve perfection. This is the reason I still play tennis. I love to hit—or attempt to hit—the perfect backhand or the perfect half volley; and yes, I admit to enjoying the appreciation of the fans for this attempt at perfection.

In track, Wyomia Tyus personifies perfection. Not just because she is the only athlete to win Gold Medals in three consecutive Olympics, but because she has been driven by her own inner chemistry to overcome so much in getting there. There are hundreds of thousands of young women running today who have the physical attributes of Wyomia Tyus. Many of these have the proper environment and opportunity to develop their talent. But only a few will have the guts, determination, and self-discipline to aim for perfection in track. They alone will succeed as Wyomia has. Hard work on the training field, good nutrition, and discipline—when combined with physical talent—will produce championship form. Those of you willing to work will profit greatly from the experience and expertise Wyomia shares with you in *Inside Jogging for Women*.

The great majority of us can dedicate our time and energy to only so many endeavors. We look at running as a supplement to our other sports programs or as a way to protect our health through recreation. For many it is a release from our more sedentary careers. *Inside Jogging for Women* lets you avoid all the pitfalls Wyomia has experienced in 25-plus years of running. Follow her advice to choose the proper warm-up exercises, training program, stretching exercises, and equipment. Only a few aches and pains must be endured. Most pains result from poor training techniques, overenthusiastic efforts, or poor equipment.

Experience, philosophy, and understanding of running are delivered in equal measure in *Inside Jogging for Women* by Wyomia Tyus. Her pursuit of perfection in track will make the way so much easier for all of us to enjoy running.

Billie Jean King

acknowledgments

Our thanks to Simone and Duane for their patience and encouragement, to Jay for his invaluable typing and suggestions, and to the women joggers who share our love of running.

I was trying to keep loose, determined not to tighten up despite the chill in the air. I kept saying, "Tyus, stay relaxed, don't tighten up. That's the only thing to remember."

I was revealing signs of nervousness so I took a deep breath, dug down inside, and found a reserve of confidence. I said to myself, "What's the use of me being nervous? They should be scared of me. I won in '64. They figure she won in '64 and she's back this year, she must still be good, you know? So let them be scared of me."

Finally I settled into the blocks, along with the fastest women in the world. It was 1968, and I was in Mexico City for my second Olympics. My coach, Ed Temple, said that when the gun sounded, I "came out like a hydrogen bomb—just one big explosive push." All I knew was that I began the race; my mind had gone blank when the starter said, "Get set." I was soon concentrating on coming out low and driving. Coach Temple recalled my race: "She stayed low for the first 10 or 12 meters and then she began to raise slowly, until she was about 20 meters out. Then she got into her regular running form, with her toes pointed straight—or maybe in just a little. She was on her toes, knees up, her body leaning at a 45-degree angle to the ground, and her arms were pumping, a relaxed kind of pumping. She was out front after 40 meters, and at the Olympic level you don't catch anyone who's leading after that. Everyone's moving too fast."

I jubilantly crossed the finish line in 11 seconds flat, a new Olympic and world record. I received another gold medal during the Mexico City Olympics as a member of the 440 relay team. All told, I have three gold medals and one silver medal. The sense of triumph was enormous, yet I can safely say I never ran just to win.

I ran because I liked it. First around

the house and then around the block and pretty soon in school. I was 13 years old, and most of my friends were in the school band or involved in some comparable school activity. Nothing interested me the way sports did so I played on the school basketball team. Soon after, I was running track, the only other athletic activity for girls. At age 15 I had begun competing, but I was continuing because I knew I had talent and it felt wonderful. I wanted to use my body and any natural skill I was fortunate enough to possess as a runner, regardless of the first places that I might garner.

I knew the excitement and fulfillment associated with running, but it was not an easy thing to convey to others. This was no longer Victorian times, when a woman would not even consider participating in an athletic endeavor, but the taboos surfaced in more contemporary terms. My mother was very confused about me, as

were other concerned relatives and friends. They were reluctant to encourage my new avocation because it seemed a threat to my femininity. I was told that the muscles in my legs would somehow prohibit me from having children! Further, it was believed that my position as a woman would be in constant jeopardy as a result of my "male" interests.

When I was scouted by a coach from Tennessee State who offered me an athletic scholarship, my interest in track became more legitimized and thus more accepted by friends and family. Tennessee State was one of the very few colleges giving track scholarships to women—athletic scholarships were almost exclusively reserved for men. It was at Tennessee that I progressed as an athlete and had the opportunity to train with some of the best women in track. Coach Temple always said, "If you can beat the girls at Tennessee State, you can beat anyone."

Our best races were against each other, and we all learned to respect the ability of other athletes. I was fortunate to learn that my confidence did not diminish when I credited other athletes, including my competitors, with their ability. A valuable camaraderie develops among athletes when they respect each other. I always felt that the runner who could accept defeat by acknowledging the winner's talent was a happy runner. No matter how fast you are, there is always going to be someone faster. Maybe not today or tomorrow but sooner than one thinks. And as for setting records, someone is always going to break them; they are there to be broken.

Growing up in Griffin, Georgia, the youngest of four children and the only female, I played and ran and combed the outdoors just as my brothers did. I am curious about what might have happened to my energy and vitality as I grew older had I not chosen the route I did. By 16 most girls have cut down on their childhood activity 50 percent. Their male contemporaries are still riding bikes, playing football, hitting a softball around, but female adolescents have become the cheerleaders watching from the sidelines. This trend continues as the girls become women and their careers and families become full-time activities. Somehow the men squeeze in the evening tennis match and the weekend touch football game, but women are still the spectators, if even that.

This is not a book on track or profes-sional women athletes, but through my experiences, at Tennessee State, in the Olympics, and later as a competitor for the International Track Association, I can draw some parallels to women and physical fitness.

Assuming that exercise is highly beneficial (and I do assume this), then women have been deprived of an essential part of life. Just as the professional woman athlete has had to struggle to display her talent with the ease and profit male athletes achieve, the average woman has had to make an extraordinary effort to get exercise without the support of others. The discrimination shows itself on all levels—the lack of athletic scholarships for women, insufficient funding of women's sports, the focus on male sports figures by the media, and a general societal conditioning that a strong and fit body is a masculine trait.

I also believe that many of the healthy (and unhealthy) attitudes toward track apply to the jogger as well. Competition, defeat, excitement, and triumph are experiences common to the runner.

Finally, I am convinced that the runner is the most physically fit of all the exercisers. The sprinter and the jogger are involved in different aspects of running, perhaps for different reasons, but their training is basically the same. They are both strengthening, firming, and limbering their bodies, as well as improving lung capacity and strengthening the heart, not to mention safeguarding their mental and emotional health.

chapter 1
WHY JOG?

Exercise can release and nourish unlimited potential for personal growth and happiness. The physically fit and athletically active person can improve his/her mental as well as physical health.

I believe these benefits are possible because the mind and the body are inextricably connected. I could be in top physical shape, but I would never have won my gold medals if my mind had not been in condition as well. Confidence and relaxation are as essential to an athlete as are strength and speed. When the body and the mind are at one with each other, the athlete's performance is more total, more rewarding. The combination of the mental and the physical can prove as important to the occasional sportsperson as it is to the professional athlete. If you want to become more physically fit, the first area to work on is your attitude.

We all tell ourselves that an integral part of being healthy is exercising, but so few of us follow through with a continued exercise regimen. We can attribute this to laziness or lack of time, but probably the main ingredient is missing—desire. Sincere and persistent desire can have a variety of catalysts.

My own desire to be physically fit originated from my love of running. The faster I ran, the more exhilarating the experience. I realized that the speed I was after came only with physical exercise and discipline. Others find their drive in a desire to lose weight, to sleep better, to discover more energy, to increase endurance, all of which can be realized through exercise. Whatever the motivation, and there are many, it will prove significant if you take the time to discover your own set of reasons for pursuing a fitness program.

Perhaps the idea of making a list of reasons for exercising or contemplating for a few hours why you want to be fit sounds a bit silly. But on those mornings when you want to sleep instead of jog, or when the soreness in your body tempts you to forego your sit-ups, or when it seems too cold out for bicycling, the desire that you took the time to tap will prove invaluable. We all need incentive to back us up when our momentum falters, and it can range from wanting to lose five pounds to wanting a gold medal at the Olympics.

It is my thesis that the mental skills involved in physical fitness are sorely neglected. It is a misconception to measure any form of exercise solely by strength or coordination. The obstacles of self-doubt, nervousness, and fear of competition are as inhibiting to one's performance as any physical deficiency. We all know people who refuse to take up tennis or jogging because they are too embarrassed to be a beginner in public. This is no small hurdle to overcome.

As important as my Olympic victories were to me, the psychological victories I have won as an athlete have been the most rewarding. I have learned how to relax and enjoy athletics so that winning becomes a result of spontaneous performance. The competitive spirit coupled with a will to win is at its best when it stems from a sense of self-worth. Moreover, losing is no longer an overwhelming defeat that discourages further enjoyment.

An important realization when you begin a jogging program is that you are working for yourself. If you keep in mind that getting fit can be a highly personal experience, eventually your self-consciousness will diminish.

As you struggle around the track, you will undoubtedly encounter a sleek figure streaking by at a pace and with an ease that seem impossible. It is worthwhile to remember at these frustrating moments that the only person you have to compete with is yourself. Furthermore, the more advanced jogger most likely has not taken notice of your heavy breathing and perspiring face. There is nothing to be embarrassed about; on the contrary, you should be proud that you are putting forth your best effort.

The traditional emphasis in sport on competition and winning needs a second, more critical look. Because of the pressures we inflict on ourselves, it is no wonder that the majority of us clutch in competition. We feel the need either to be better than someone else or to impress someone else. The crucial mistake is that a person or persons other than ourselves become the criterion for defining our self-worth.

It saddens me to see friends take up a sport or exercise for health and enjoyment and ultimately succumb to the competitiveness so rooted in this society. I knew a woman who was in the process of reevaluating her life. She decided to take up tennis in order to get regular exercise and to add to her recreational activities. She began playing at a country club where it soon became apparent people were measured by their skill on the court. There was a great deal of status attached to those who played on the A team and, of course, to the club champion. My friend soon became susceptible to the club's standards and felt inferior because she was a beginning player. Unfortunately, she was so intimidated by the competition she gave up tennis—it was no longer the fun sport she had pursued at the outset.

Another friend had approached me about getting into shape. I suggested a daily jogging program, to which she reluctantly agreed. I sensed that the program would be difficult for her simply because she was so hesitant to give it a try. In other words, she had not discovered that all-important desire to back up her fears. Sure enough, she was embarrassed in front of a high school track team that practiced on the same track. She bought an expensive warm-up suit in hopes that the other runners would be impressed. She went so far as to leave soon after anyone approached the track because she was sure it would be noticed that she could do only a quarter mile without stopping.

Both friends suffered far more damage than the relinquishment of their chosen forms of exercise. They joined the forces that rate the value of a human being by how well he or she performs. They sacrificed pleasure for frustration; relaxation for anxiety.

None of us can always be a winner. Therefore, if winning is the only thing that makes practice and discipline worthwhile, one is certain to suffer great disappointments. I felt excitement and satisfaction when I won my races, but coming in first was never my reason for running—it was more of a fringe benefit. Trophies are not given for effort, which, as far as I am concerned, merits recognition as much as winning. To insist on being a winner or the best at anything you do is to set impossible standards of excellence. But to insist on giving your best endeavor is to set a reasonable goal.

Physical fitness is not easily achieved. I suspect that a great many people consider themselves fit when, in fact, they have not begun to attain what they could in that direction. Perhaps I am belaboring the idea of complete fitness, but when I use the word, I am referring to the entire human being. One's ability to live a full, active, and stress-free life is, ideally, the outcome of a physical fitness program. Of course, a program with such far-reaching goals must be an ongoing process. Ultimately, the fitness regimen I envision would be an integral part of the daily business of life. Once a fitness program fits comfortably into the normal routine of your life, it becomes less of a burden and more of a pleasure.

Physical exercise can provide an emotional outlet for the problems of daily life.

Further, it can enhance one's self-esteem, contribute to the relaxation of one's mind, and provide a focus for concentration and challenge.

Consider the woman who is home most of the day occupied with children and the maintenance of a house. She undoubtedly has a busy day full of tensions and hassles. She cleans the house, runs errands, does laundry, chauffeurs children, cooks meals, and if she is lucky, sneaks a few moments to herself. Between the drudgery and the routine there are probably warm, rewarding moments, but these can be rare. This woman needs to do something solely for herself. Aside from the obvious health benefits, I believe she could find great personal satisfaction in jogging. It is time totally devoted to herself; it is time outside of the house; and it is time spent accomplishing something.

The woman who goes off to an office every morning has her own set of pressures. She has the mental tensions of a career, the pressure to succeed, the hassles of a bureaucratic organization, and the relentless race for money. Of course, she has her satisfactions, too, but she needs an outlet to something simple, something done purely for enjoyment. Jogging can be a way to unwind from the pressures of a job, a way to relax and have fun. There is a steady rhythm to running that makes it a natural to clear the mind. While running, it is surprisingly easy to forget the problems and the complexities of business and to simply experience the marvelous effect that exercise is having on your body.

I have a friend who is a successful executive who enjoys and thrives on her work. Unfortunately, the tensions of her position took their toll and she developed a severe ulcer. Medication and an appropriate diet were prescribed, but the job proved a constant source of aggravation. Her doctor, an avid jogger himself, suggested that she try running every evening so that she could have a focus outside of her work. After a few months on a jogging program, she was hooked. She actually hurried home from the office to jog and found the exercise a remarkable way to relax. Her ulcer improved rapidly, and although she is still a workaholic, she is healthy and better equipped to handle pressure.

Among working and nonworking women, married and single women, young and old women, there are women who are insecure and unchallenged. To say that jogging and exercise are the answer to their happiness is to oversimplify the situation. But to credit jogging as an activity that builds confidence and provides challenges is, I believe, a fair accolade.

We all must deal with failures and disappointments in life, and any chance to succeed, even if it means running a mile without stopping, is a welcome addition to anyone's day. Jogging is a tangible challenge that can build confidence and provide satisfaction. If, for example, the challenge is to lose weight or firm up one's body, then continued jogging can bring concrete results. Perhaps you found that you could not jog a half mile. After a week of combined jogging and walking, that half mile can easily be conquered. Another person's goal may be to note evident progress each week or even each day of a jogging program. It is exciting how rapidly the body strengthens during running, increasing one's distance each day. If done consistently, jogging also becomes increasingly easier and the pain quickly diminishes.

Everyone wants to look and feel attractive. Jogging can create a physical change in the body, and through that change can emerge a happier person. When you are running regularly, your body becomes firm and taut. Even those who do not usually lose pounds will often have their weight well redistributed. Complexions become clear and rosy, and even eyes tend to be brighter and more alert. Joggers are known to be sound sleepers, and a well-rested person looks it. The active, exercised person looks better and consequently feels better about her self-image. It is not stretching the point to say that jogging is capable of tapping confidence, fulfillment, and a generally positive outlook on life.

Physical fitness is important to everyone. I cannot emphasize enough how much easier it is to cope with life's stresses when one is feeling healthy and attractive. As a woman, I feel especially inclined toward encouraging women to discover the power within their bodies. Too often the woman is the spectator of a male involved in sport. Until recently she seldom was involved in the sport herself. I am dismayed by fitness books with chapters specifically for women in which exercise time is cut in half and only "soft" exercises are illustrated. Indeed, women have some catching up to do in the area of fitness, but the exercises that provide the optimum results for men do the same for women. There is no sound reason for instructing men in the art of jogging and women in the art of walking. Certainly, the amount of exercise and the rate of progress should differ according to individuals. But the fact remains that some exercises are better than others, and everyone should be encouraged to participate in those.

One of the physical activities I admire the most is dance. Dancers are involved with the total use of their bodies. Many of them run or swim to increase their endurance; they have to be extremely limber to perform gymnasticlike moves; they exercise to increase muscle strength needed for leaps and supports; and they perfect grace so that the piece is aesthetically pleasing and responsive. Men and women alike aspire to use their bodies to their fullest potential. I am not advocating that the average person try to be as disciplined as a dancer but, rather, that the body be approached as the multifaceted, complex tool that it is.

While I prefer active exercise to static exercise, I think that they can complement each other. For example, swimming is an active exercise, increasing lung and heart capacity, but calisthenics can strengthen arms and legs used in swimming. Similarly, yoga, a static exercise, is advantageous when used in conjunction with jogging or bicycling. Although static exercises are necessary to warm up the body and to tone muscles, they will not make one physically fit by themselves.

Active exercises are also referred to as aerobic exercises. This means that they benefit cardiovascular endurance, or increase oxygen transportation and utilization. Extreme effort of short duration is known as anaerobic exercise. This is an exercise, like a wind sprint, that requires speed rather than endurance. It can also enhance an aerobic activity but alone does not provide fitness.

I know many men who are body builders. They faithfully perform isometrics, calisthenics, and weight lifting. Sure enough, their chests grow massive and their muscles abundant. But what about their heart, their lungs, their blood pressure? If I needed a physically fit man or woman for a job, I would not hesitate to choose the jogger who appears slight of build rather than the muscle-bound weight lifter. Of course, a static exerciser is better than a nonexerciser, but he does not merit the physically fit label. I believe in getting in touch with the whole body, like the dancer. This means working toward strength, flexibility, and stamina. Each attribute of fitness has its own set of exercises, and they work best when blended into a balanced program.

Exercise is essential for optimum physical and mental health. Our ancestors needed physically fit bodies to stay alive. Their typical day involved 12 to 14 hours of hard labor, during which they struggled against the very environment that was their lifeblood. We still have the same body, designed for physical activity, as did ancient man. Unfortunately, the contemporary world no longer demands that we use our bodies. We must recognize that the ordinary tasks of daily life do not provide enough exercise to develop and maintain good muscle tone and cardiovascular fitness. A conscious exercise program is necessary to combat the sedentary routines and effort-saving conveniences of our daily lives.

About 55 percent of the deaths in the United States result from cardiovascular diseases that are directly associated with obesity and inactivity. It is clear that physically active people are less likely to experience heart attacks or other forms of cardiovascular disease than sedentary people. An active person who does suffer a coronary attack will probably have a less severe attack and will be more apt to survive the trauma.

Physical activity is as important as diet in maintaining proper weight, and being overweight is directly related to disease and shortened life expectancy. Some medical authorities believe that life expectancy decreases approximately one percent for each pound of excess fat carried by an individual between the ages of 40 and 50. Weight reduction and maintainence can be accomplished by a reasonable increase in physical activity, such as jogging.

Physical exercise enables the entire body to function more effectively as it stimulates various organs and systems.

Posture can be improved through exercise like jogging that increases the tone of supporting muscles. This decreases the frequency of back pain and other discomforts.

Strength, or the ability to exert force against resistance, is necessary not just for those who do difficult muscular work. We would all be better prepared to meet various daily trials with increased strength. Once again, developed and maintained strength requires an exercise program.

Muscle tone, strength, and endurance can be developed with the right kind of jogging program. Physical activity can increase the reserve capacity of the heart and stimulate blood circulation so that the various organs of the body are more adequately supplied with blood, oxygen, and energy fuel. This process results in less fatigue and greater stamina.

In an inactive person, the blood vessels in the muscles become narrower, which means the heart has to work harder to pump the blood through them. When a person exercises, the blood vessels in his/her muscles expand greatly. Because the blood can now be pumped more easily through the larger pipes, exercise reduces the strain on the heart and may even cause a drop in blood pressure. This is why jogging is an excellent protection against heart disease.

Exercise must be of sufficient intensity and duration to benefit the cardiovascular system. These variables are directly related to the attainment of cardiovascular endurance. The intensity of an activity can be measured by your heart rate.

As the intensity increases, so does the heart rate. Duration refers to the amount of time spent in active exercise. An increase in these variables will increase cardiovascular endurance. The effectiveness of an exercise can be determined by the amount of constant exertion it requires. The exercise should have a duration well over five minutes, and the heart rate should be between 130-150 beats per minute. Jogging is the best example of an exercise with more than sufficient intensity and duration to greatly improve the cardiovascular system.

I am selling jogging and physical fitness in general as one might sell a bottled elixir, but my pitch is not exaggerated. I sincerely believe that a balanced, thorough exercise program that involves jogging can have far-reaching consequences. It is my hope that these pages will supply a guideline and encouragement for exciting personal discoveries. When your attitude is one of confidence, enjoyment, self-respect, and enthusiasm, jogging can become one of the most genuinely special aspects of your life.

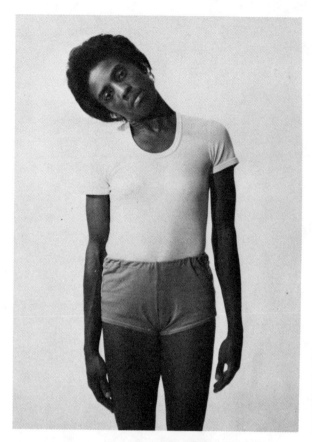
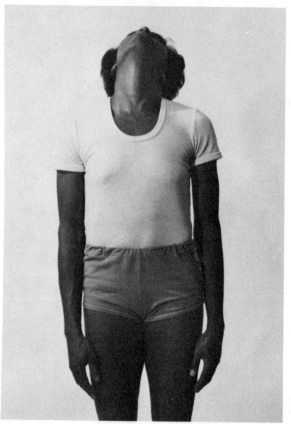
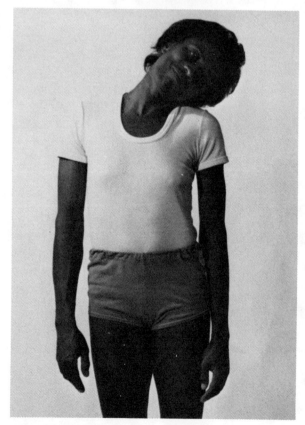
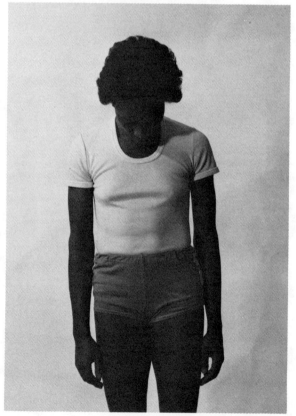

NECK ROTATION.

chapter 2
GET SET

Once the desire and the motivation for jogging have been tapped, you have crossed the most difficult hurdle. The proverbial first step being the hardest, hundreds of rewarding miles can easily follow. Hopefully, you are eager to start running, but some practical measures must be taken to ensure a safe and beneficial workout.

The first step is to have a thorough physical examination. An increasing number of physicians are encouraging their patients to run, and a good many are jogging themselves. Your doctor can often be helpful in designing an appropriate jogging program for you, paying special attention to your heart and lungs. Age, weight, and the general health and condition of a runner have obvious effects on the success of a jogging program. A doctor's encouragement and/or caution should not be taken lightly and should be determined before the program is begun.

The next consideration is the proper running equipment. Above all, a good pair of running shoes is basic and essen-

tial. Now that jogging has become so popular, there are dozens of shoe manufacturers making it easy to find a well-made running shoe.

When shopping for shoes, pay close attention to the heel structure. A jogger needs substantial heel padding—at least one-quarter to one-half inch—to absorb the shock of the foot hitting the surface. While sprinters run toe to heel, joggers run heel to toe and therefore need the extra support in the heel of the shoe. (If a sprinter falls back on her heels, she will inevitably run slower, while a jogger cannot stay up on her toes without getting sore.) The shock absorption factor is more important to the jogger than speed. An average jogging shoe should weigh 10 to 11 ounces.

The shank of the shoe, the area under the arch, also must absorb the surface impact. It should be built solid and firm.

Try running shoes on with socks and move around in them in the store. Obviously, your feet will be moving around a great deal in the shoes so feeling them while sitting in a chair is not much of an indication of their quality. While the design and the structure of a running shoe are extremely significant, comfort and a good fit are most important. Above all, buy a pair that *feels* good.

Warm-up suits, like running shoes, have kept pace with the jogging boom. They are well suited (no pun intended) to jogging in addition to being attractive. However, a sweat shirt and sweat pants can serve the same purpose with less expense. The warmth that both provide helps protect the muscles and prevents pulls. On a warm day shorts and a T-shirt are adequate, but if there is a chill in the air or any dampness, a sweat or warm-up suit is advisable.

Socks should be worn to prevent blisters and chafing, though some veteran runners with toughened feet can safely go without them. A sweatband is helpful to keep the salt sting out of the eyes, and hair out of the way.

With your doctor's OK in hand and clad in the latest jogging fashions, you are probably itching to pick up the pace, but the most important preparation is yet to come—warm-up exercises.

Women have been consistently superior to men in an important area of fitness. They are usually more limber than men and thus have greater ability to stretch muscles. Many hulking football players would find it difficult to execute some of the following stretching and warm-up exercises. Their training is geared toward increasing their strength and speed, often at the neglect of keeping their bodies limber.

Limbering is especially important for the beginning exerciser because it cuts down considerably on soreness the day after. I warm up before every run even though my muscles are already well stretched. Preliminary exercises are like a tune-up; they keep the body in good working order so that the more active exercise that follows has an operable base from which to work.

Minor aches and soreness are often experienced by the beginning exerciser. Do not be alarmed by this unless severe muscle strain or dislocations occur. It will not take long before you know how to pace yourself with the warm-up exercises as well as the jogging. Exercises that involve stretching need to be done on a regular basis, but you should not push too hard, too fast. It takes time for the body to become limber, and it should not be forced into difficult positions prematurely.

Stretching exercises should be practiced in the smoothest manner possible. Move gently with an even flowing motion. Never jerk the body in an effort to force the stretch. Although exercising and jogging may seem a far cry from dancing, it is precisely the grace inherent in dance that I am talking about. If the exercises are done evenly and gracefully, the body will be more relaxed, allowing the stretch to happen. On the other hand, if there is a violent motion to the exercise, the body will immediately tense up and will fight the stretch.

You may be wondering how to possibly perform a sit-up or jumping jack gracefully! It is largely a matter of body awareness. For example, if you concentrate on the structure and the feel of your back, you will be less likely to slam your back down to the ground during a sit-up. Rather, you will focus on letting each vertebra, beginning with the lower back, hit the floor in succession. The result is a less violent, more flowing back motion.

Another helpful method is to adapt a graceful image to an exercise. For example, imagine yourself to be in water when performing jumping jacks. Your arms and legs should move as if part of a swimming stroke and thus more slowly and evenly. Water is often a helpful relaxation image. During exercise, the shoulders tend to rise up and get extremely tight. If you concentrate and imagine water cascading down your shoulders, you may be surprised how easily they release the tension.

Always remember to balance your exercises. If you do an exercise to stretch your right leg, do the same stretch on your left leg. You will probably notice that one side of your body is more limber than the other. Resist temptation to work solely the limber side and give the stiff half attention as well. Also note that your body will be stiffer in the morning than in the evening. This does not mean that you should not jog in the morning but rather, that your body may need some extra warming up.

The following exercises are geared for the beginning through advanced exerciser. The difference lies in the difficulty and ease in doing the exercises. Simply, the beginner should start slowly, listening to her body to discover its limits. The advanced exerciser can and should do more and extend herself to the fullest degree.

These exercises are designed to work the entire body for suppleness and strength. If you incorporate these exercises or some of your own into your jogging program, it is helpful to do the same warm-up each day. If you maintain consistency, you will be able to gauge your progress, which can be very satisfying. It also is important to perform a systematic, disciplined, and balanced set of exercises.

NECK ROTATION

Lower the right ear to the right shoulder; lower the head backward; lower the left ear to the left shoulder; and move the head forward with the chin to the chest. Repeat, doing the rotation slowly at first so that you can feel the pull in your neck. Then proceed to gently roll the head in a circle and reverse. In the beginning it is likely that you will hear a cracking noise

in your neck as you do the rotations. In a few weeks, as the neck becomes more mobile, the sound will be gone.

FORWARD DROP

Bend forward slowly from the waist, tucking your chin toward your chest. Relaxation is important so do not push to the ground. Instead, allow your own weight to drop you lower. Let your arms dangle and concentrate on keeping the back of the neck relaxed. Breathe in and come up slowly. Repeat five times, breathing out as you go down. Each day you will notice your hands getting closer to the ground. If you are able to touch the floor, hold in that position for a few moments for an excellent leg and back stretch.

STANDING TOE TOUCH

This is a variation of the forward drop in which you stand with your right leg over your left leg. Keeping your legs straight, bend the trunk so that your hands grasp your ankles. Keep your head down and your neck relaxed. If you feel a severe pull in the backs of your legs, do not bend as far forward. Repeat with the left leg crossed in front of the right leg. This will stretch the muscles, ligaments, tendons, and nerves of the back and legs.

ARM CIRCLES AND CROSSES

Raise arms straight to the side. Rotate the arms in large circles, slowly making the circles smaller. Reverse the rotation.

Move arms in a crisscrossing motion in front of the body. The right arm crosses over the left and then the left crosses over the right. The shoulder joints will soon loosen up, making it less difficult to keep your arms extended.

TRUNK TWIST VARIATIONS

Hands on hips, legs apart, bend trunk to

FORWARD DROP.

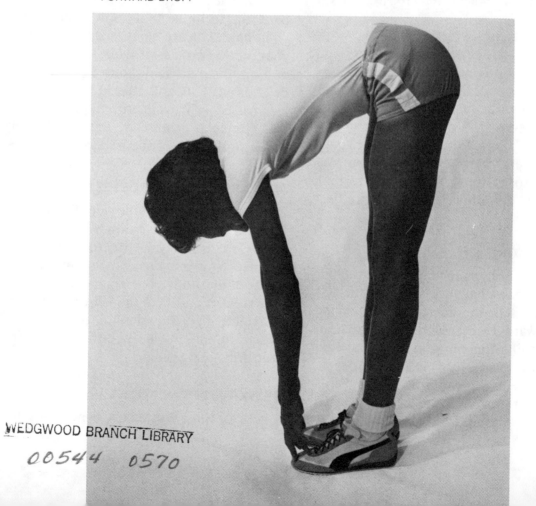

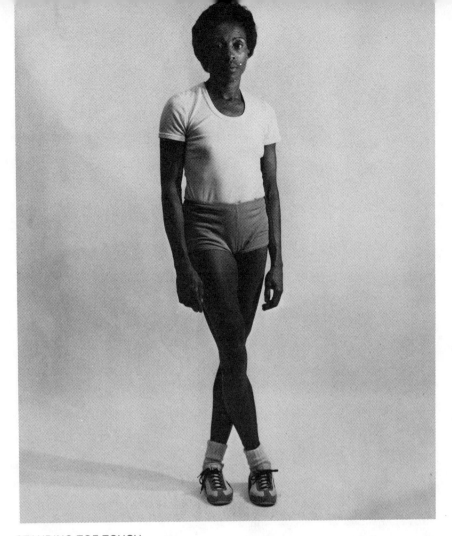

STANDING TOE TOUCH.

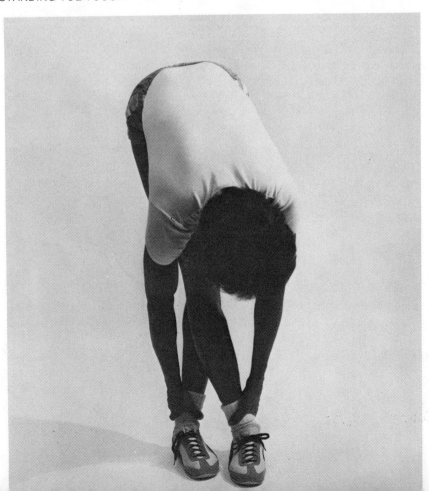

(ABOVE) ARM CIRCLES. (Below) Arm crosses.

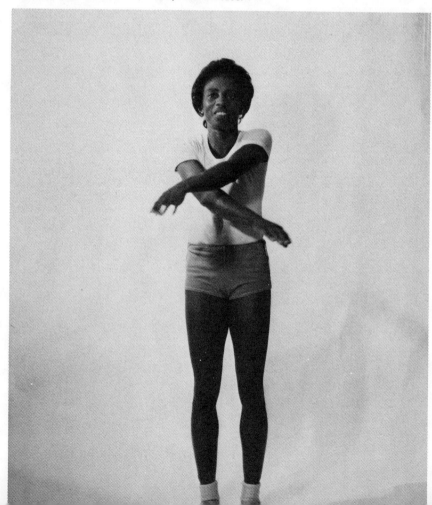

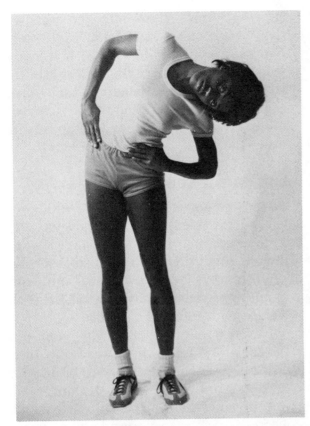

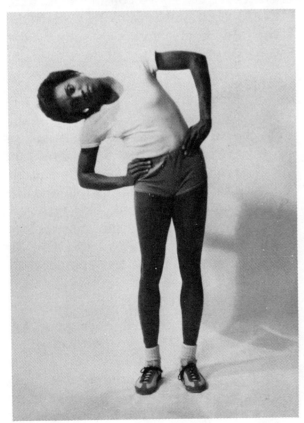

TRUNK TWIST

the left; bend forward; bend trunk to the right; and bend backward with only a slight arch in the back. Repeat, beginning with the bend to the right side. At each position you may *gently* bounce so that a stretch can be felt on your opposite side.

Now bend the trunk to the left but leave the left arm down at your side and bring the right arm over your head, forming an arc. Once again, gently bounce so that the stretch can be felt along your side. The same exercise can be done without the bounces, allowing your weight to do the work. Repeat on the right side.

WINDMILL

This exercise is similar to the forward drop, but it involves more movement. Stand with your feet about 3 feet apart, arms out to the side. Touch your left toe with your right hand; touch your right toe with your left hand. Repeat.

HANDCLASP

Clasp hands behind your back with your arms straightened and flexed up and away from your body. This manner of flexing helps limber the shoulder joints and upper back muscles. It also expands and stretches the ribcage and lungs.

STRETCH SPLIT

Stand with your legs spread three feet apart. Bend your left knee, keeping your weight over your left foot. You may place your hands on your knees to help keep your balance. Keep your right foot flat on the ground. Repeat exercise on your right side. You should feel the stretch on the insides of your thighs and in your calves.

WALL STRETCH

Stand three to four feet from the wall with your arms stretched straight forward toward the wall. Place your left foot flat behind your right foot, heel down, toes straight ahead. Lean into the wall (or tree, chair, etc.), stretching your lower posterior leg. Hold for 30 to 60 seconds. Repeat with other foot. Repeat the stretch, this time bending each knee slightly and exaggerating the stretch even more. Hold 30 to 60 seconds. Repeat with other foot.

SITTING TOE TOUCHES

Sit on the ground, back erect, with your left leg extended and your right leg bent at the knee, placing the right foot against the left thigh. Bend forward so that your head touches your left knee and your hands are stretched toward your left foot. Repeat with right leg extended.

Now extend both legs with your feet flexed away from or toward the face. Grasp ankles and *gently* try to bring your head to your knees. Most beginners will not be able to do the complete bend. These exercises give considerable stretch to the back and legs so in a short time you will be able to touch your head to your knees.

FOOT FLEX

This is an easy yet beneficial exercise that anyone can do. Legs extended, make a fist with your hands and flex the toes and feet back toward the chest. Spread the fingers as far apart as possible and flex the toes and feet forward. This exercise is effective in loosening the muscles and nerves in the legs. It also helps maintain good circulation in the legs and back.

OPEN LEG STRETCH

Sitting on the ground, open your legs anywhere from three to five feet apart. The wider apart, the better the stretch, but beginners should do only what feels comfortable. Bend forward over your left leg, bringing your head to your knee, arms extended. Hold five to ten seconds. Repeat the stretch over your right leg. Bend forward between your legs, keeping

TRUNK TWIST variation with arc.

WINDMILL.

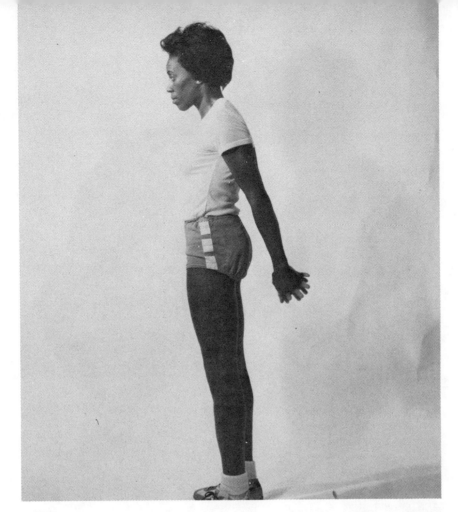

HANDCLASP

STRETCH SPLIT.

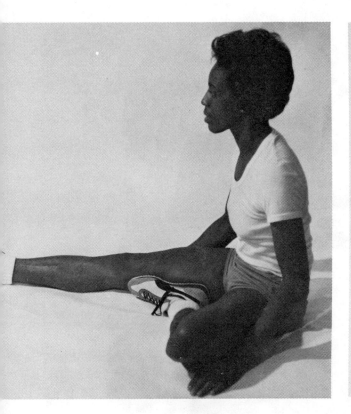

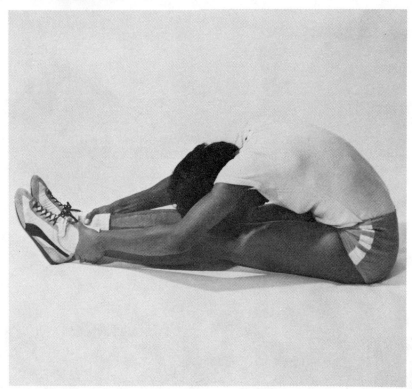

SITTING TOE TOUCH.

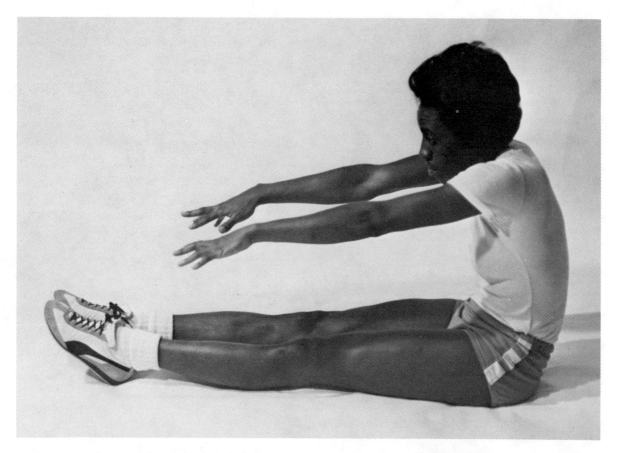

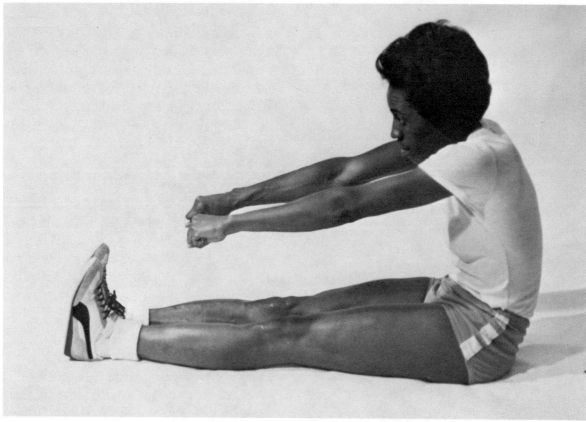

FOOT FLEX.

the back of your neck relaxed. This stretch is more difficult than the one over your legs, and beginners should use appropriate care.

LYING KNEE PULL

Lie flat on your back with your arms to your sides. Breathe in and reach around your left knee, bringing it up to your chest. Hold for five to ten seconds. Exhale slowly and straighten the leg. Repeat three to five times with each knee. Now bring both knees to your chest and hold for five to ten seconds.

STANDING KNEE PULL

This exercise involves the same action as the lying knee pull, but it is done in a standing position. Stand with your right foot firmly planted on the ground, leg straight. Raise your left knee to your chest, your arms clasped around the knee. Gently pull the knee toward you, keeping your back erect. Repeat with the right knee.

THE PLOW

Lie flat on your back, arms to your side. Slowly lift your knees toward your chest. Roll backward until your weight is behind your head. Straighten your legs and try to touch your toes to the ground behind you, heels pressed gently to the floor. Beginners may find it necessary to keep their knees bent. Your hands can either remain at your side or support your back. This exercise puts a tremendous stretch on the back, the legs, and the back of the neck. People with any back problems should attempt this posture with caution.

SITTING HURDLE

This exercise is similar to the sitting toe touch. With the right leg extended, bend the left leg behind your back so that your left foot is up against the buttocks. Gently

bend forward over your right leg, your arms extended toward your right foot. Repeat on other side.

STANDING HURDLE

Place your left knee flat down on a waist-high surface. Keep the right leg straight and slowly bend your trunk over the right leg. Repeat on other side. Try to keep the back of the neck relaxed during this exercise, which is basically a standing variation of the sitting hurdle.

INDIAN CURL

Sit cross-legged with your back relaxed. Concentrating on relaxing the back of the neck, bend forward with your hands flat on the ground out in front of your body. This can be a very relaxing position if you let your weight drop forward.

TREADMILL

Get into a push-up position, with your hands braced on the floor perpendicular to your shoulders, the buttocks even with your back. Both legs should be bent one behind the other, only your toes touching the ground. Push off and bring one leg forward as the other goes backward. This is good for the blood circulation and strengthens the feet and legs.

SIT-UPS

Almost everyone is familiar with sit-ups. They should be performed only with bent knees, the elbows coming forward to meet the knees. This position reduces the strain on the back, still helping its flexibility. The sit-up is also an excellent stomach strengthener.

SHOULDER STAND

This exercise takes the same position as the plow, but the legs are held straight up. When you begin to roll your weight back, lower your elbows and shoulders to the

(PAGES 24 AND 25) Open leg stretch.

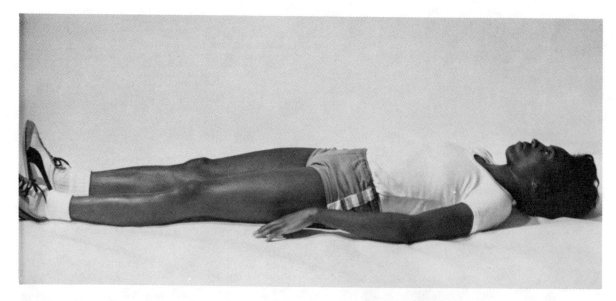

LYING KNEE PULL.

STANDING KNEE PULL.

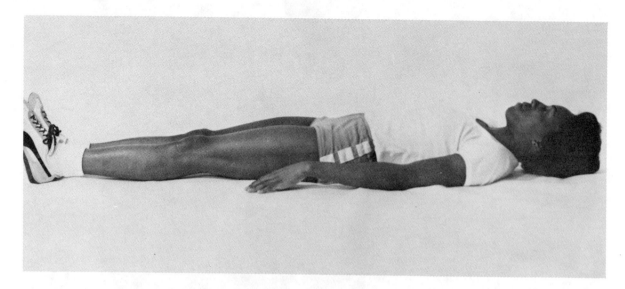

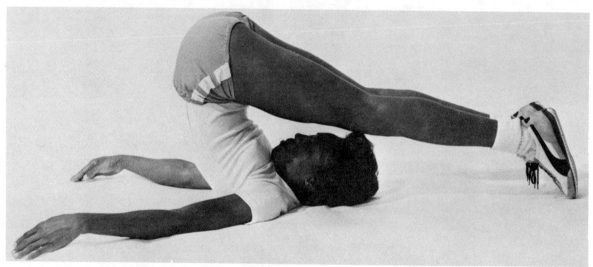

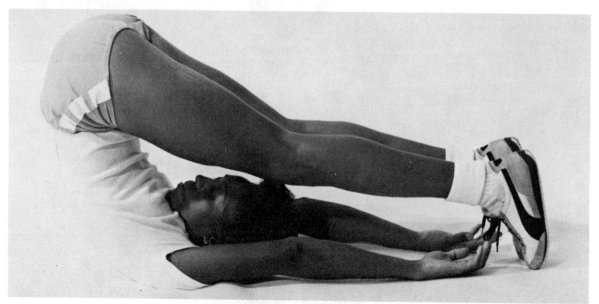

THE PLOW.

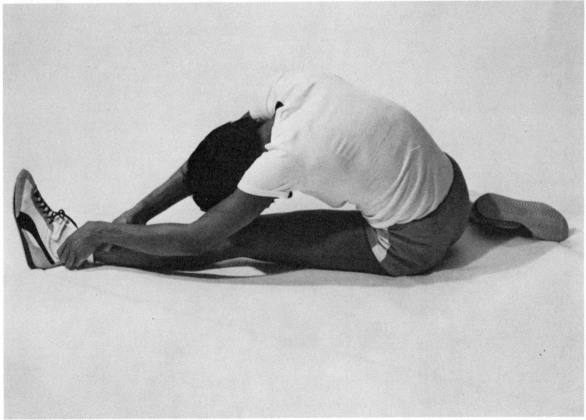

SITTING HURDLE.

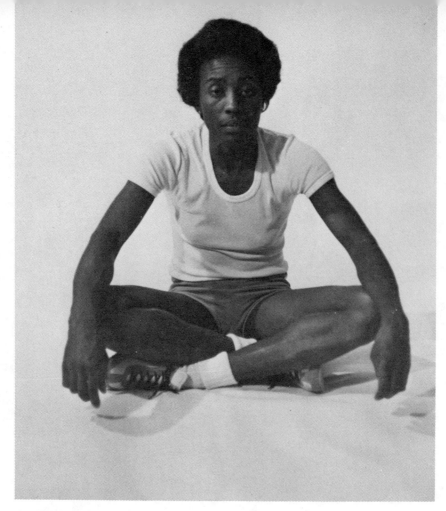

INDIAN CURL.

TREADMILL.

SIT-UP.

floor for added support. Allow the momentum from the rolling motion to carry the feet all the way over the forehead. The hands should slide under the lower back and support the weight of the hips. Then straighten the legs so that your body forms a straight line from the shoulders to the feet. Hold this position for 30 seconds. Relax and take the position again. This position reverses the blood flow from the legs into the chest, neck, and head. The increased supply of blood and oxygen to these areas helps eliminate fatigue. The neck is also strengthened and its flexibility increased.

Well-known exercises that need little explanation, such as jumping jacks, push-ups, and chin-ups, should also be added to your warm-up routine. These provide strengthening and conditioning.

Knee injuries, shin splints, Achilles tendonitis, and a variety of pulled muscles tend to plague the new runner. If warm-up exercises are followed daily, there is very little chance of these injuries occurring. If injuries still occur, chances are they are due to some imperfection of the foot. The discomfort of foot injuries is rarely confined to that part of the body. They affect especially the knee, the hip, and the shin. A podiatrist (doctor who treats feet) should be seen to treat any possible congenital foot defects.

One of the most common and painful injuries to the runner is the shin splint. This is an extreme soreness between the shinbone and the calf muscle. Poorly fitting shoes used on pavement are a prime cause of shin splints, as is an insufficient warm-up. The best cure is rest coupled with massages, hot baths, and whirlpools if possible.

Pulled hamstring muscles are also a problem to the runner. These muscles extend the thigh at the hip and flex the leg at the knees. This injury should not happen to the jogger unless she is accelerating too fast or doing hard sprints.

Various other muscle pulls plague runners. Ice wrapped in a towel should be applied to the sore area to prevent swelling. Heat treatment should be applied at least 24 hours after the injury occurs. Anywhere from one to seven days' rest may be needed to cure a muscle pull, but you should resume running as soon as possible. If you stay away too long, you will have to work twice as hard to rebuild all your muscles. If the pain of any injury is severe and/or persistent, see a doctor immediately. Remember, a thorough warm-up session prior to jogging is the best preventive medicine.

The importance of food should not be ignored. It is a popular and accurate belief that you are what you eat. It would be incomplete to exercise your body and disregard what goes inside it. Just as jogging is an excellent defense against disease, fatigue, and depression, nutrition, too, has a strong impact on health. Like exercise, the nutrients from food affect virtually every function of the body.

I am hesitant to prescribe a structured diet for joggers because I believe that eating habits are highly individual. Even the diehard junk food addict will find herself eating better when she begins to jog. An organic process takes place when you are involved in consistent and active exercise. You naturally crave healthful foods and a sensible diet because they make the running easier and more rewarding. Your body rejects junk food because it simply does not do anything for you. It is a common misconception that the sugar in a candy bar or a piece of cake will give the extra energy you need to exercise. On the contrary, that sugar will be used up rapidly, and your body experiences a low energy point soon after. Avoid quick nonnutritive snacks before you run. Instead, eat a piece of fruit or drink a glass of juice. It is wise to eat nothing for at least two hours before you jog because it takes that long for your body to digest its food properly.

It is helpful for joggers to have a

(PAGES 34 AND 35) Shoulder stand.

knowledge of the basic nutrients and their food sources so that they can incorporate those foods into their diets.

PROTEIN

Every cell in the body needs protein, which plays a significant role in the structure of cells, body tissue, and enzymes, the regulators of body processes. It is indispensable to life's continuing cycle of growth and restoration. Milk and its products, meat, poultry, fish, eggs, and nuts are good sources of protein.

IRON

Iron functions in the red blood cells to carry the oxygen from the lungs throughout the body. Anemia is caused by an iron deficiency. Women of childbearing age need almost twice as much iron as men because of the iron lost during menstruation. Liver is an excellent source of iron, as are meat, green leafy vegetables, egg yolk, molasses, and whole grain breads and cereals.

FATS

Fat tissue serves as a source of fuel that can be used for energy as the body requires it. It is also utilized to transport fat-soluble vitamins, such as A and E, throughout the body. Fat is important to the body as a heat insulator as well and serves as a cushion for the protection and support of body organs. Everyone needs some fat, but an excess can be detrimental. Our diets are too frequently high in fats, and a fat-rich diet should be avoided.

CARBOHYDRATES

Carbohydrates are second to fats as the main fuel source supplied through food. They are utilized as energy sources mainly by the nerve tissues. Excessive amounts of carbohydrates can be converted to fat and are often the source of weight problems. The American diet is heavy on carbohydrates, as it is on fats. The main sources of carbohydrates are fruits, pastries, and varied sweets. Your sources of carbohydrates should be chosen carefully and kept under control.

CALCIUM

Calcium is the main builder of bones and teeth and also acts to repair them when necessary. It is used in normal muscle, heart, and nerve function and in blood coagulation. Bone diseases can occur as a result of calcium deficiency. Milk and its products and dark green leafy vegetables are excellent sources of calcium.

IODINE

Iodine is essential for the formation of the thyroid hormone. Most people meet their iodine requirement through iodized salt. The main natural source of iodine is saltwater fish.

VITAMIN A

Vitamin A contributes to eyesight, especially night vision and color vision. Some of the best sources of vitamin A are liver, yellow fruits, and dark green and yellow vegetables.

VITAMIN B$_1$ (THIAMINE)

Thiamine plays an important role in the release of energy from food. Consequently, the amount of thiamine the body requires depends on the amount of food eaten. Thiamine is widely distributed in foods so it is easily acquired in the diet. Although thiamine is removed from grains during processing, it is added back in enriched products.

VITAMIN B$_2$ (RIBOFLAVIN)

Riboflavin has a similar function to thiamine, and the amount required is also dependent on the amount of food eaten. The best sources are dairy products. Like thiamine, this nutrient is also added in the enrichment of bread and cereal products.

VITAMIN C (ASCORBIC ACID)

Man is one of the few species that cannot synthesize their own vitamin C. Because the body does not store this vitamin, it is important to include it every day. Ascorbic acid assists in the formation of bones and teeth. It also helps promote the healing of wounds. The best sources of vitamin C are citrus fruits and their juices, green leafy vegetables, potatoes, tomatoes, broccoli, cabbage, and green peppers.

A recent law required that all foods be labeled as to their nutritional value, which is presented as a percentage of the U.S. Recommended Daily Allowances. It is important to pay attention to these labels and eat accordingly. A healthful diet will contain a balance of required nutrients. The body's need for protein, carbohydrates, fats, vitamins, and minerals should be obtained through a variety of foods—dairy products, fruits, vegetables, breads and cereals, lean meat, fish, and poultry.

Although some people notice a loss of appetite when they are jogging and exercising, the majority of active people find that their appetite increases in proportion to the energy expenditure during exercise. Do not be concerned if you find yourself eating a bit more. This seems to be the body's way of balancing intake with output, thus maintaining its own weight. If you are interested in losing weight while exercising, you should maintain your normal intake of food while allowing for an increase in activity. You will most likely exercise away some of the extra fat tissue.

Ideally, the energy, or calories, expended for body activities should equal the food energy consumed. When more food energy is consumed than is used for activity, the energy is put into storage in the form of fatty tissue. This extra fat can be eliminated by increasing the energy expenditure so that it is greater than the food energy consumed. The body will be forced to use its stored fuel to meet its energy needs.

It is very difficult to experience a significant weight loss without increased exercise. Moreover, a loss resulting from exercise is more likely to be a lasting condition. Jogging requires a large caloric expenditure and significantly affects the caloric balance.

It is very likely that other unhealthful habits besides those associated with eating will also naturally be eliminated through jogging. It is largely a matter of attitude, and presumably if you are embarking on a jogging program, you are attuned to health. Your body will send signals that will be difficult to ignore. Running is a cleansing process that eliminates poisons from the body and discovers energy and strength. If you are a heavy smoker, your body will fight those damaging substances. If you are a heavy drinker, your body will have to struggle that much harder to overcome sluggishness and headaches. I am not suggesting that joggers live the life of deprivation; only that you be sensitive to the awakening in your body as you begin to jog. Let any new habits come about largely naturally, because that will be far more satisfying than following some rigid program that you chart before you start running.

THIS IS AN example of correct running form.

chapter 3
GO...!

Jogging is not as complicated as competitive sports—there are no fouls, no penalties, no points, no score. There are no rules aside from some practical and healthful concerns. Jogging is a simple and natural form of exercise that anyone can perform. It would be doing jogging a disservice to concentrate too much on technique. Once your feet take flight, your body naturally takes a form all its own. There are no points for aesthetic or stylish qualities. Everyone looks different running, and runners are even known to develop certain eccentricities in their styles. If you start asking yourself how to put your feet down or what to do with your arms, you may disrupt the natural flow of the movement. The smoothness and easiness of the run are important. Breathing should come naturally as well. Inhale and exhale deeply at whatever rate is comfortable. Like your stride, your breath will develop its own rhythm.

However, there are some fundamentals of correct running even if "correct" covers a wide range of differences and varies from person to person. By correct, I mean a form that makes jogging a healthful, relaxing, and injury-free experience. It is important to do what comes naturally as long as it is mechanically sound.

Running is a complete, flowing movement. It is composed of independent action by the feet, legs, arms, hands, head, and shoulders. To improve the overall running form, it is necessary to examine these separate parts. But once you have the mechanics down, it is important to think of the action as an overall movement. It is a complete cycle of motion consisting of alternating support on the feet. In other words, the rear foot bears the weight of the body and pushes the body into a position where both feet are off the ground. The front foot is then planted on the ground, supporting the body weight before pushing both feet off the ground again. If the cycle is com-

PROPER FOOT placement for jogging.

pleted smoothly until it becomes one movement, the run acquires an even rhythm that actually helps boost speed and distance.

Posture should be the main stylistic focus. The trunk should be carried in an upright position, with the feet moving as part of a line of progression. The runner who leans forward or to the side is fighting gravity and causing a lot of unnecessary work. The ideal posture is upright and relaxed, with your back perpendicular to the ground. This form permits easier use of the leg muscles and helps in taking air into the lungs.

The pelvis is the key to the proper posture. It should be brought forward in relation to the rest of the body. The pelvis aids in straightening the spine and thus maintains an upright position.

The chest should be flat rather than protruded. The buttocks should be tucked under. This will aid in keeping the back straight. Do not, however, assume a posture as if you are at attention. This will cause you to puff out the chest and pull back and tighten up your shoulders, resulting in a reverse curve in the back.

It is necessary to lean when you are climbing a hill. A slight forward tilt will give your stride the extra power to combat a steep terrain. Avoid the tendency to lean backward while going downhill and keep the torso perpendicular to the ground. It is clear that aside from hills, the less of a forward lean of the body, the greater the efficiency of the runner. Energy is not wasted lifting the body forward with every step.

Runners should plant the foot on the outside edge and then roll it inward, resulting in increased shock absorption. The point of impact is increasingly forward on the foot as the runner picks up

CORRECT FORM for running uphill.

DOWNHILL RUNNING FORM.

FOOT PLACEMENT.

speed. The jogger, who is less concerned with speed than the racer, should land first on her heel. The next point of contact should be the balls of the feet, ensuring a safe landing.

The stride is dependent on posture and the position of the feet, If your feet are well planted under you and your posture is correct, the stride will happen by itself, allowing for individual style. For the most efficiency, there should be no pronounced knee lift or kickup at the back. If you allow your legs to move naturally, this will probably be avoided. The faster the pace, the more outstretched your legs will be, but a relatively short stride in which the leg is not fully extended is most effective for distance running. Remember to keep on top of your feet. Your foot should strike *after* it has reached the farthest point of advance. The point of contact between your foot and ground

should occur directly under your knee, not out in front. If you keep your knees bent and do not overstride, this will happen naturally. You will be able to feel if you are making contact correctly because if your foot hits the ground ahead of your knee, the leg will be too straight; it will act as a brake instead of an accelerator.

Your arms and hands, often taken for granted in running, have important functions. If your hands are tense, they can trigger a chain reaction, tightening up the rest of the body. Many runners make the mistake of clenching their fists or of opening their hands with fingers outstretched. Both positions create tension in the hands and arms.

The most effective hand position is a loose fist. Your thumb should be placed on your index finger, with fingers lightly clenched and your palm slightly turned

CORRECT JOGGING STRIDE.

up. The hands should be relaxed but *not* limp. The wrist and the elbow also tend to turn rigid, and although they should be held firm, they should be relaxed. A locked elbow greatly inhibits movement and causes the shoulders to move around. The elbows should flex so that the shoulders can remain inert and parallel to the ground.

The arms combine with the leg movement to create the rhythm of the stride. They swing much like pendulums moving straight ahead. The swing should not be exaggerated so as to waste energy. The greater the speed, the greater the arc the arms will make.

The head and the shoulders are the most common areas of tension. If your posture is correct, the head should sit right. However, the muscles at the base of the neck may still tense up. The jaw muscles and the muscles around the eyes also need to be consciously relaxed.

The best way to check your style is to focus on a mental picture. Think tall, as if you are being lifted out of the pelvis. A helpful image is that of a marionette. Picture a string attached to your head and someone up above gently pulling it straight. Most important, think light. Imagine yourself barely skimming the surface as you run *over* the ground. The

GOOD SPRINTING STRIDE.

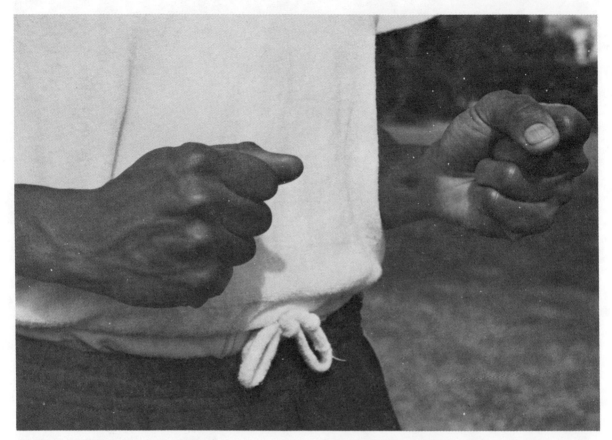

(ABOVE) AN EXAMPLE of a tight clenched fist. *(Below)* Good hand position.

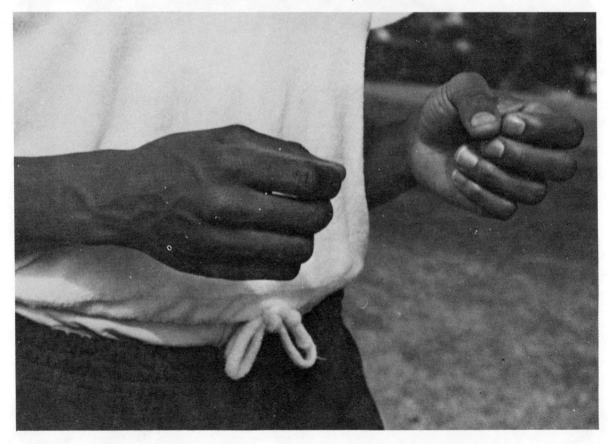

(ABOVE) HOLDING TENSION in the neck, face, and shoulders. *(Below)* Proper relaxed head position.

advantage of quality shoes is that they make it easier to run lightly. If your feet are making excessive noise as they meet the ground, you are not lifting up or running *on* the legs. Pounding unnecessarily jars the body and causes the otherwise smooth rhythm of jogging to be interrupted by bouncing and swaying. It is also a cause of shin splints.

Occasionally check the common tension points—the shoulders, the neck, the face, the hands. At first you will notice that these areas are tight, but if you continually let them drop whenever your attention is brought to the tension, you will learn to run relaxed. If you spend the first few months of jogging thinking about style and relaxation and making an effort to improve in these areas, you will be guaranteeing yourself years of unconscious enjoyment. Many experienced runners speak of an altered state of consciousness during running. Their bodies are accustomed to running long distances at good paces in correct form. The mechanics come so naturally that they pay no attention whatsoever to how far they are running or how fast. They may have run five to six miles before their minds switch back to what they are doing. The experience can be highly pleasurable and the ultimate in relaxation.

The beginner who has never jogged before and is probably out of shape needs to develop her strength and endurance gradually. It is essential that you do not do too much too soon. A combined jogging and walking program is the best way to condition a body unaccustomed to aerobic exercise. I have suggested that the beginner progress to a one-mile jog in four weeks. It is possible, however, that this rate of progress will vary according to an individual's physical condition and determination. The following progress rate disregards the time required to cover the distance. It is the continuous, gradual, and steady increase in distance that is important.

Day 1.   Jog 110 yds.; walk 110 yds.; jog 110 yds.; walk 110 yds.; jog 110 yds.; walk 110 yds.; jog 110 yds.; walk 110 yds. Although alternating with walking, you will be jogging a total of a quarter mile. (If this feels too ambitious, jog only a total of 420 yds.)
Day 2.   The same as Day 1.
Day 3.   Jog 220 yds.; walk 220 yds.; jog 220 yds.; walk 220 yds.
Day 4.   The same as Day 3.
Day 5.   Jog 440 yds. (a quarter mile); walk 440 yds.
Day 6.   The same as Day 5.
Day 7.   Jog 550 yds; walk 550 yds.
Day 8.   The same as Day 7.
Day 9.   Jog 660 yds.; walk 660 yds.
Day 10.   The same as Day 9.
Day 11.   Jog 770 yds.; walk 770 yds.
Day 12.   The same as Day 11.
Day 13.   Jog 880 yds. (This is a half mile of running, and the walking equivalent can be optional.)
Day 14.   The same as Day 13.

Continue adding 110 yds. every other day until you reach 1,760 yds. or one mile. It takes about two months to jog a mile with regular and relative ease. Up until that time, accomplishing the mile will probably take a great deal of effort. Suddenly the day will come when you have no doubt as to whether you can jog a mile, and you feel able to go farther if you want to. If you know that you can do at least an additional quarter mile, you are securely and steadily jogging the one mile.

When you have accomplished the "secure mile," it is reasonable to work on time. There are some workouts often used by track people that can also be used by joggers who want to improve their speed.

INS AND OUTS (INTERVALS)

These are done best on a track where you can measure distance easily. Run at a sprint pace (on your toes) 100 yds. of a

FOR SPEED DRILLS, the runner stays on her toes.

straightaway section of the track. Walk briskly 110 yds. of the curve. Run another straightaway and walk another curve. Now do the reverse so that you are running the curve and walking the straightaway.

HIGH KNEES

This drill is almost like running in place, but you are moving forward. Run 50 yds. with your knees coming up toward your waist. Take short, quick strides. If you perform the high knees with an erect back, you will probably have good posture when you jog.

VARIED PACES

Run a mile total while alternating between sprint, jog, and stride paces. Keep

the sprints to 100-yd. bursts and then recover with a few hundred yards of jogging, eventually moving into a slow stride before sprinting again. It is easier on the legs to do this drill on a grassy terrain.

These speed drills are completely optional and should be attempted only by the conditioned jogger. While it is important to increase pace, this will happen naturally the more you jog. If you jog a mile over a period of months without increasing your distance, your mile time is bound to pick up. Similarly, if you move on to two miles, you can maintain that distance until you feel yourself jogging faster. Timing yourself is an excellent incentive to run more at a greater intensity. It is a tangible record of progress, as is increased distance or increased ease.

Where you jog is a personal decision. If you have the proper shoes, any surface is

HIGH KNEES.

safe, though pavement should be avoided if possible. Some runners prefer running on a track because they can gauge distance easily. A 440 track is especially helpful when you are building up to the mile run. Other runners choose to run on grass, while some take to the streets. A quiet, scenic route can make running more enjoyable, and I always encourage people to try jogging in the woods, in a park, or on a peaceful country road if at all possible.

JOGGING CAN BE fun with friends and pets!

chapter 4
A SOURCE OF HAPPINESS

Jogging should be a fun addition to your life. It is hard work, but through that hard work you are creating an ability that did not exist before. The athlete has often been likened to the artist, who through hard work experiences the joy of creating a process as well as a result. Through concentration and determination, the jogger is *earning* her sense of satisfaction and accomplishment. If jogging is only a grueling, boring routine, it needs to be reexamined. There are ways to make running the happy, fulfilling experience it can and should be. Runners may not boast wide grins as they jog by, but the good feelings are expressed in a sort of inner smile.

A fair indication of the joy that jogging brings are the "running addicts." Everyone I know who has been jogging for at least six months and stops sorely misses it. Even if they miss a day, these runners somehow feel cheated. It can be rewarding to record daily running mileage on a visible calendar. You can look at tangible proof of your progress. Chances are that if you see a series of blank days on the calendar, you'll feel the loss and rush out for a hearty workout.

The convenience of running only adds to its enjoyment and its accessibility. Running is the most inexpensive aerobic exercise I know of. Aside from a good pair of shoes, which is a lasting investment, running is free. Running can also do the most for you in the least amount of time. Getting places can be seen in terms of exercise—jog to work, to school, to the store, to a friend's!

Some factories and production plants have even provided employees with tracks and other exercise facilities. They recognize that a healthy, happy employee will demonstrate more of a commitment to the job. Jogging can be done in the minutes before work or during a lunch hour.

Marathon running is a popular source of motivation and reward for the amateur

KEEP IN STRIDE—jog for life (Photo
Bonnie Schiffman).

A QUIET RUN alone (Photo: Bonnie Schiffman).

runner. There are an increasingly large number of marathon races exclusively for women. Accomplished women marathoners are becoming well-known names to running buffs. To qualify for a marathon, one has to be in excellent condition, and to finish a marathon takes even greater effort. But any marathoner will tell you that the exhilaration after a race is well worth the training. Marathons have attracted many over-forty women, who have their own categories in many of the races. These women are embarking on a new and rejuvenating experience at a time in their lives when they thought "you couldn't teach old dogs new tricks"!

Because of different psychological characteristics, I think that women are more

SHARING THE JOYS of jogging.

able to look at jogging as a source of fun and happiness than are men. While women usually begin jogging for health and enjoyment, men, who have always been instilled with competition, tend to jog as a means to excel. Perhaps it is because women have traditionally been less achievement oriented than men that they can transcend their ego and discover further pleasures in running. This does not mean that women do not have the capacity or will to compete and succeed but, rather, that they can *also* find their rewards in sheer enjoyment.

Running alone can be extremely therapeutic. It can be a time to work out problems or simply a time to be by yourself. When you run alone, you can truly concentrate on the personal satisfaction of feeling your body work, sweat, and move. Running with a friend or a spouse or a child can be enjoyable, too. It is a way to share a mutually rewarding experience. Many joggers like to run with their dogs; dogs benefit from the exercise, too!

Wherever you run, whatever time of day, in whatever make of shoe, the evidence is abundant that jogging can increase the quality of life. Imagine how exciting it would be to have a built-in source of energy, confidence, fun, and health, and then go out and jog! Women everywhere are discovering the joys of running and the new life-style it brings with it. The jogging boom offers women a new awakening to the realms of fitness. The mastery of the forces within their minds and bodies enables women to have a deeper awareness of themselves and their potential.

MOTHERS AND DAUGHTERS can enjoy jogging together.

index

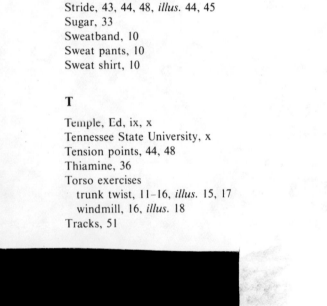